The Burning of Troy

Also by Richard Foerster

Transfigured Nights (chapbook)
Sudden Harbor
The Hours (chapbook)
Patterns of Descent
Trillium
Double Going

THE BURNING OF TROY

for Karen,
with salutations
for you & your writing

Poems by

RICHARD FOERSTER

Richard Foerster

11.8.06

AMERICAN POETS CONTINUUM SERIES, No. 100

BOA Editions, Ltd. ❧ Rochester, NY ❧ 2006

First Edition
06 07 08 09   7 6 5 4 3 2 1

Publications by BOA Editions, Ltd.—a not-for-profit corporation under section
501 (c) (3) of the United States Internal Revenue Code—are made possible
with the assistance of grants from the Literature Program of the New York State
Council on the Arts; the Literature Program of the National Endowment for the
Arts; the County of Monroe, NY; the Lannan Foundation for support of the Lannan
Translation Selection Series; the Sonia Raiziss Giop Charitable Foundation;
the Mary S. Mulligan Charitable Trust; the Rochester Area Community Foun-
dation; the Arts & Cultural Council for Greater Rochester; the Steeple-Jack
Fund; the Elizabeth F. Cheney Foundation; the Chesonis Family Foundation;
the Ames-Amzalak Memorial Trust in memory of Henry Ames, Semon Amzalak
and Dan Amzalak; and contributions from many individuals nationwide.

Cover Design: Geri McCormick
Cover Art: "The Burning of Troy" (detail) by Jan Brueghel the Elder, ©
ARTOTHEK, Munich, Alte Pinakothek
Manufacturing: BookMobile
BOA Logo: Mirko

Library of Congress Cataloging-in-Publication Data

Foerster, Richard, 1949–
   The burning of Troy : poems / by Richard Foerster.
      p. cm. — (American poets continuum series ; no. 100)
   ISBN 1–929918–83–6 (alk. paper)
   I. Title. II. Series: American poets continuum series ; v. 100.

PS3556.O23B87 2006
811'.54—dc22

BOA Editions, Ltd.
Thom Ward, Editor
David Oliveiri, Chair
A. Poulin, Jr., President & Founder (1976–1996)
260 East Avenue
Rochester, NY 14604

www.boaeditions.org

NATIONAL
ENDOWMENT
FOR THE ARTS

State of the Arts

NYSCA

CONTENTS

III

❦

for Kevin Richard
in memory of his father

I

Gentle Adonis is dying, Cythera;
what shall we do?
                              —Sappho

. . . the blank tearless gaze . . . was fixed
on that incomprehensible contradiction
between memory and nonexistence.
                              —Proust

OCTET

It started as a racket, teased into poised
play: eight soot-sheened grackles,
amid the wing-flare and flutter
of their tails. They tiptoed above
the sprucetops with minute adjustments
to negotiate the wind, beaks thrust
seaward, certain as weathervanes
on steeples. They settled with the resolution

of a diva's fan snapped shut,
and it seemed the day has been assembled
just for them, at the tap of some
invisible baton, as if, there on my knees
among the weeds that had overtaken
the garden, my hands rank with earth,
I'd been summoned to attend those birds,
pinnacled and buoyant in their ease,

as if something more should lie beyond
that chance uplifting of my eyes
from a neglected chore, something
in the *check, check, check* of their calls—
a counterpoint, a rhythm, a rondo
unfolding from within their rasps
and rusty whistles—if only a few concerted
moments of pure, unwilled forgetting.

For as long as I could bear to listen,
I sensed a music, harshly patterned,
but one that even a constricted throat
would try to give voice to, make it
human, though nailed to pain:
There is no death in this world
of beauty. No life you cannot pluck
back out of thinnest air.

YORKE WOODS

Those summers, before he'd arrive
home from work, I'd lie in the self-
indulgent tumult of the hot tub

and wait, sprawled skyward,
for Arcturus to wink from its gap
high in the overarching oaks,

for dusky blue to deepen
deeper, and sing in my lolling
Come, pipistrelle, mein Fledermaus,

invoking the familiar to appear:
a lone dustman sweeping
the roofline. Summer by summer,

my thoughts sputtered up
to join that winging loyalty
as its black scallops sculpted

the blackening air, and I'd feel
my flesh loft into the ease
of evenings while suppers

simmered on the stove. A haunting
metronomics kept, it seemed,
the ratcheted coil of the planet

running sure—and that life
I had, akin to marriage.
So what must I make of the season

I found that bat crumpled
like a chamois, soiled and stiff
on the dew-wet lawn? And him

our brightest
star

just hours later, dying? Our house-
hold broken like a string of beads,
that tub soon drained and sold?

Nights now when I pass, moths
ghost the air, tilt blindly at
each radiant, curtained pane.

AN ABIDING

The day the x-ray showed his lung ghost-laced
with fluid, a carrier pigeon came to rest
in the small delta of the woodland garden
we'd wedged against the forest, and forage awhile
beneath the hanging feeder and ornamentals
we'd hoped might thrive for years in dappling seep-
ages of summer light: A pure extreme,
a white so milk-souled only its eyes' black
beads and an azure ring on its left foot
seemed to wed it to this world. A cipher,
from where, for whom, whose paraclete
nearly fearless as we peered from the living
room window? Each thread of reason frayed
and snapped with unbearable possibilities.
All that week—in the limbo of waiting, as
we learned the arcanum of disease, its likely
crabwise crawl through ever-deepening burrows,
thinking to prepare for the worst will make
it easier when it comes—there in the garden
that stark and wayward mystery lingered among
the blood-red rhododendrons, and when we knew
finally, we saw from the shadowed window
where we stood in long embrace, trembling,
the bird was gone, and all around would be
as it had been, for better or for worse.

ARTICHOKE

For all the bother, it's the peeling away
we savored, the slow striptease
toward a tender heart—

how each petal dipped in the buttery sauce
was raked across our lower
teeth, its residue

less redolent of desire than sweet restraint,
a mere foretaste of passion,
but the scaly plates

piled up like potsherds in a kitchen midden,
a history in what's now
useless, discarded—

so we strained after less and less as the barbs
perhaps drew a little blood
and we cut our way

into the core to rid us of the fiber
that would stifle every ut-
terance between us.

In our quest for that morsel,
how we risked silence,
risked even
love.

DRUM

"If this is to be my fate. . . ,"
he began, just days before
the ashen pallor, the zephyrs

of tanked air he'd crave,
but I'd started to drum the taut
blades of his back as we sat

on the green sofa and gazed
out at the heat-stunned
blue hydrangeas—an easing

primal melody, his lungs
beneath already desert
lakes, storm-flooded,

the long dormant now
sudden, unstoppable,
a teeming with life I imagined

palpable there below each
fingerwhorl. The gentlest
patter boomed like thunder,

and whatever words passed
toward those blue hydrangeas
only one of us could hear.

VIGIL

As I slept in that last room at the end
of a corridor's plasticizing light, beside him,
where monitors peeped like famished birds
and the clepsydra of morphine dolloped its mercies,
the CD I'd keyed to *repeat* scattered
crumbs of forest sounds deeper
and deeper along the paths of dream.

Lost in that foliage, its densities lit
by a black sun, I grew aware
my breathing had stepped into sync with his—
not like sprinters neck-and-neck,
nor marathoners in steadied pace,
more a pair of bellows: prayerful
puffs tempoed to keep a shrinking

clutch of kindling aglow. Faithless
apostle, I hovered in quasi-sleep
around that point of light, the pulsing
tidal flow, the small expense
of air, till a gasp like sudden gold
flooded me back to the charred,
lapsed logic of that room.

SPOONS

In the momentary convex
gleam of one stainless
steel spoon held hot
from washing, the stippled damp
wiped all at once clear
with a cloth, just as the hand
begins to ease down toward the tray,

how grief can shimmer up
through such idle motion—
how the weight of a left arm
draped over another, as a finger
seeks to feather a nipple
into flame, can seem six-
feet's worth of dirt atop

a ravaged cage, while lungs
struggle beneath to find enough
breath to say *No, I can't
breathe like this*—then as quick
all slips into place, rattling
an instant before that silence
after the drawer's slid shut.

SMOKE

: that which things go up in : the after-
chain of incandescence : his lungs'

coiled nebulae : the space between
particulates : dust & seed-stars

flung then funneling : the infinitesimal's
unconfined chaotic : cells bombarded

to opacity : that chasm, there, exposed
: the fact of him, split & splintering

: a spigot's hiss & boil : the mist
beneath a mask : what he existed in

: that oxygenated rictus : the chug & spew
behind a racing engine : the terminal

achieved : my meniscus of memory : the face,
a smudge now nightly risen into dream

SETTING OUT

. . . the accumulated life, its omnium
gatherum, the rubble of over-
stuffed drawers upturned, picked
through like berries, bagged and hefted
to the curb—so much to foist

on Good Will: the long-laundered,
care-kept, the now threadbare
that few would wear: fading
hand-painted Ts of tropic isles,
one blazoned *Love like a volcano*.

What should your son want to keep
of you? Already he's stripped away
the paper from the walls, slathered
the rustic wood a Turneresque tint
of daffodil. The rooms erupt

with absolute erasure. I leave
with what is mine to claim, gifts
of fifteen years, the weight of never
imagining them back, my slow steps
from the door. Someday, I know, I'll set out

our two Tundra Glass goblets, stare
into the perfect torsion of their bowls,
the love-knot illusion, and see a face
not quite yours come filtering back
through the wine's molten glow.

TITHONUS

Sarcophagus of morning : marbleized air :
apples studding the abandoned orchard : same
torch song year after year : reds & greens : stop : go :
the hillside's spill to shadow : quick rill & slick
stones' slow erosion : an equation for *yield* :
goldenrod : hawkweed : touch-me-not : prods toward sense-
less defiance : crizzling frost on the seedpods :
the wind's tiny detonations : & always
this aurora : the infinite gradations :
a closed set : the stunning thought : the barb I scrape
repeat repeat : sarcophagus of mourning :

IN DREAM

—that percolation of the sleepless brain
up from the sump of our days' drainings,

in its sift of shifting time and places,
where memories' brokers trade, in ever-racing

speculation, our securities and bonds,
in that refuge of fears and longing beyond

logic and the senses, in its cold, crepuscular
light, the haunt of all our muscular

dead—I watched again the unraveling
bandage of his breath, how it traveled

on the air awhile, a fraying banderole,
till the words inscripted on that scroll,

their delicate freight, mouthed but voiceless (like his face
when I stretched to kiss it), dissolved without a trace.

❧

AUBADE

Still, the house; then light-crack, the entr'acte
  of dawn: each pane laliqued, fern-etched
      on the emery-wheel of December. Brief,
that film, already burning, the evaporate fact
  I'd stay lost in longer, the farfetched
      dream the sun now filches like a thief.

And so the windows fill with day's contusions,
  a slurry of routine, hours stretching
      toward predictable horizons. Belief
once fluttered at my lips. What god can soothe
      such grief?

A POT OF CROCUSES

The weathered crocus pot, which I coddle
each winter under salt marsh hay,
again commands its center stage
in my kitchen window. In terraced beds,
the corms poke through the soil
like randy waking gods, their pale
phalluses swelling in the sun.

All morning I reveled in the comfort
of this ancient ritual till my neighbor's
scab-kneed boy on Easter break
began to trundle up and down
the street on his skateboard, trying
to gain the necessary speed
that could springload him into air,

as if in that moment he would escape
once and for all the tedious maze
of his adolescence and return, perfect
and unbloodied, to an earth remade,
invincible with flowers. So I watched
in secret, and found myself urging
him on, but soon he slouched off

with raw, abraded palms toward home
and I felt I needed to call him back—
my not-quite budding Adonis—
but could see on the asphalt beneath
my window the small red stains
from his hands, and I wanted to say,
Here, take these crocuses

to your mother, so she might forgive
the scarring a woman has to endure
to see a boy safely to manhood.
Instead, I stood there, wavering
with that crowded pot of spikes in my hands,
and knew if I had summoned him
it wouldn't have been for any promise

of beauty I had to offer, nor any
incorruptible idea of it,
nor even the cherished terra cotta
I've buried and retrieved these fifteen
years. For how could I have looked
him in the eyes, not knowing which
of these must end up broken first?

❦

AIX EN PROVENCE

. . . and then the world arced open
like a door, a blue ventricle

pulsing with muscled flow,
yet the space between my heart

and brain seemed a suitcase
stuffed with shadows, a gorged

terrain of misunderstanding.
Along those ancient stuccoed streets

the windows were iced with summer
blaze above swarms of red

umbrellas—so many medusas
casting about their tresses of shade.

And the snipped sycamores squatted
like green hens on Cours Mirabeau,

where I brooded over my own
clutch of regrets while the bistros'

cranked awnings lowered
their indifferent lids. A waiter

swept from Les Deux Garçons,
out to a table for one. His cloud

of pastis pearled around
a single cube. Across my knees

a creased white napkin spread
like a map in all directions.

I stared as pigeons scoured
the pavement: *Where to? Where to?*

🌿

WINTER SOLSTICE: NEWGRANGE, IRELAND

We crouched to sidle through the passageway,
up to the chambered crux of the tomb,

and stood within the corbelled hive,
knowing that soon a beam would creep

as far inside the dark as we had gone.
On that brief, honeyed shaft of dawn,

the Neolithic builders believed the souls
of their dead would swarm back out to life.

Such was the weight of their faith
that they spent decades in the long drone

of hauling two hundred thousand tons
of riverstone up from the snaking Boyne

to that hilltop circle, mounding it acre-wide.
Surely, even then, after they'd shuffled back

into the brilliant day chaffed with frost,
the worry of the wind again began to nag

at their ears as they squinted into the full blaze
of that so calculated orbit and struggled

in their measured circumspection to heave
the far greater weight of lamentation into place,

tethered, as it must have been, year after year
to that momentary, near-blinding thread.

MARIONETTE

From the starboard bow, I watched
the silent gesture of the wake
unfold, expecting an infinite

breadth as the ferry churned
hard to the west. Out from La Digue,
on cobalt depths, the hull rolled

in the swells, and my shoulders
sank then rose as if beneath
a prayer shawl. In the silence

of that gesture, my small plea
heaved into grief when the wavering
trace of our passage faded,

far to this side of sky. Rocked
in that bow, I nodded, a wooden
dumb assent, my lips drawn

tight as that distant line
which now seemed a smirk across
the face of things, till the ferry

angled slow toward Baie Ste. Anne,
and two flying fish sheared
the air, two arcing sparks

in tandem, horizon-aimed,
and in that winged transit
I glimpsed all I wanted of heaven.

STONE

But for the thirteen letters
of his name and the chiseled
dates that a hyphen spans—

as if it were the only
vital bridge between
two chartless lands:

those vast oblivions
of before he was and after—
I might mistake this granite

for something winter heaved
carelessly into the thawed
New England light, a stepping-

stone in mud season, yet one
a farmer would nevertheless take
a shovel to, as would I

were it not so precisely set
flush with the green earth
and I could undo the mason's marks.

II

Can there be history without resentment?
—Larissa MacFarquhar

SAMSARA

It's come to this:
the past must be

my present tense,
the heavy hum

rising from the lotus
pond, its mucked

bed, the sunlight's
glancing blows,

here, and here
again, reverberant

as gongs. That portal
spreads like thighs:

for lips, a head,
the umbilicus trailing

a flagellum's thrash—
a firmament smeared

with stars. Even now
the Southern Cross

hovers like a kite
above the unsuspecting

day. That wheel,
that gap on which

it soars, what light
penetrates?

COWRIE

Erosaria caputserpentis

I found a cowrie, rolled in the spent
surf of last night's storm, a star-etched
firmament I cupped in my hand. It bore
a fawn-brown glaze, smooth and scrotal
to the touch—a boy's innocent store
of treasure. A flip of the shell and I exposed
the cleft, serrated edges like a maw,
dentata, as if Freud himself wielded
the burin at its design.

          And I recalled
how I once circled and recircled a life-
sized sculpture of Hermaphroditus,
how I was held in its orbit at first
by the artist's trick of change: one body
fused in love's embrace, a youth
felled by passion's sword, the ardent
jut between his legs, till halfway round
began the gentle rise, a girl's soft hips
and tumbling hair—each solid form
eclipsed by another unbecoming.

          And there
in my hand, as I dipped the cowrie
back to water, the primitive slug stirred
within and spread its tarry black
mantle across my palm, insistent
as any fear I ever drew from the deep.
Then like a lotus closing, it enfolded
the shell—a coalescing, slow awareness
of inertial need, ignorant of the burden's
worth and why its every neural urge

secretes such hard beauty—like a belief
our bodies wear the wheeling sky for skin.

🌿

AMONG THE DAUGHTERS OF LYCOMEDES

Too young to cross the street, where boys
my age crouched with toy guns
sparking from between parked cars
and tossed their flesh-pink rubber Spaldings,

I remained this side, obedient beneath
my mother's unblinking window
to spend the summer days at jump-rope,
safe among the traffic of girls.

After supper, but long before the sky
would settle like a shroud upon my bed,
I'd lie awake, hearing the divided
laughter from the games in the street below.

And years later, alone outside a foreign city,
I'd recall their names, my bitter
lullaby hummed to the strains
of a never-quite-sexless innocence:

like Rosemary when she squatted to pee,
that lingering perplexity at my first
shuddery glimpse of absence;
or Cathy wiping sweat with her shirt,

the coppery penny-sized nipples
no larger than mine, the longed-for
kiss, a flirting with misunderstood desire.
That abyss I longed to cross would stretch

the length of the street for years, and so
I learned to jump and master the extremes
of Double Dutch and girlish poise within
the confines of the ropes' helical blur—

a momentary weightless space where
grace and speed might yet deflect
the taunts of boys, so unlike me then,
as now, still yapping at my heels

on nights the neon smolders through the drapes
and rumpled sheets define a plain
where every battle I hoped to win
was settled in that distant pattering spin.

🌿

EARLY AND LATE

1

Southpawed, I sat in St. Brendan's first-grade class,
at a wrought-framed desk, hands primly folded
atop the gouged, graffitoed hardwood lid that bore
the dark veneer of all the other straight-backed,
uniformed boys who'd passed that way before.

Too unschooled for pens, I'd set my fat, blunt-leaded
pencil in its shallow trough, the red shaft scarred
with the pit-marks of teething. All black and white
against the chalked blackboard, Sister taught
the rigid curves and angularities of early ABCs,

but I, true to some time-tested prejudice,
was the sinister recalcitrant, her only devil-
handed boy she placed, cowed and cowering,
closest to her desk so that when my left hand
would reach, by instinct, for that instrument of self-

expression, I'd feel her wooden knuckle-raps and bear
my red Fs home. How many pencils did I sharpen
into extinction, practicing what seemed a secret code
I longed to break, enjoined as I was—though I couldn't
grasp it then—in the ardor of apprenticeship?

2

What flows now between the mind-
forged nib and the paper's pure
vacancy: these vagrant trails,

blue-black as night, stipped
with distant glimmer, jots
and tittles, the deep dye

of being, cursive, connected,
stroked, and curled, the flourish
of a word—there!—like a whip

inked into meaning.

᭢

MINOTAUR

A maze, into which
eyes, peering,

must adjust: a door
latched, and another,

then one left open for
the as-yet timid

to enter, dim-lit
as the dead, wandering,

girded in white chitons,
as much the uniform

here as silence:
the cul-de-sac

these men seek
for thundering hearts,

each trailing his thread
of yesterdays, to ravel

a way out into light,
to whatever he thought he was

before fingers began
to smell of semen and sweat,

before his throat swelled
in unenunciated prayer,

that gurgle of remembering before
the past snaps like string.

POOLSIDE IN PROVINCETOWN

I couldn't help scrutinizing the faded
inks he wore like a manifesto, fleshed-out
constellations that floated on pallid skin:
His arms were skulled and daggered;
twinned sibilant bolts zagged his thighs;
and through the thicket of his chest, hooded
ember-eyed knights peered. His pierced nipples

doubled as shields bossed with pink suns.
Within the cloaks' deep folds, the cross wavered
like flames when he laughed, seeing me cock my head
to read the scripted Gothic motto that arched
round his belly's sunken grotto: 𝕬𝕽𝖄𝕬𝕹
𝕹𝕬𝕿𝕴𝕺𝕹. I don't know when exactly
I loosened to his barleyed charm, but soon

I was swigging beers, able to imagine him clothed,
less a stranger than close acquaintance, feckless
as my uncle in Hamburg when I was eight,
unwrapping like a sacred totem the ribboned
medal the Führer gave my grandmother
"for bearing eighteen pure Aryan children
to the Reich." How my mother beamed,

"It proves the family is not Polish, but Prussian."
That stylized eagle somewhere still clutches
in its talons the broken cross I thought was a sin
even to jot on paper. Now there, against the pool's
blue tiles, amid the playful chaos of that young man's
plashing feet, just above the anklebone—
those four radiant gammas seemed to spin

like an Old World windmill's vanes set
to some slow, relentless grinding task. Miraculous,
what survives, like those sibling aunts and uncles

beneath the Allies' firestorms, only to emerge
unscathed from Gomorrah's strafed shelters.
And my mother, secure in her white gloves
and postwar hats in the Bronx. When did I

finally understand the import of that scarred
silence the day she hurried us off the bus
after I asked, pointing, why the man beside me
had numbers on his wrist? This other one, too,
caught me, mutely staring, but had no ill-fitting
sleeves to tug, nothing at all to hide,
no gesture I might misread as shame.

❦

TRAINING FILM, 1967

When I think on how my body loves,
how the reined discipline of desire
can be so casually unbridled,
I find myself with an adolescent's

pulsing confusion, back in that spring
our cassocked teachers marched us, mute
soldiers of Christ, well prepped
in devotion to stand, blue-

blazered in the sun, stiff as the effigy
we came to honor. Eight hundred
boys arrayed on the campus quad,
we'd thumb our rosaries' black beads

through fists as if cocking and recocking
rifles to the tempoed drone
of our Hail Marys. How I hymned
the Virgin's praise, lost among

those coltish voices, leaping up
in chords embarrassing as acne.
All that May, summer loomed
with redemptive promise, ticking down

through exams and valedictions, fittings
for the big tuxed night of the prom.
And sex lurked deep in the amazed
gropings of the mind—a place

our teachers feared they'd never delve
except by projecting the blatant blood
of troubled births: that film of breached
flowerings and episiotomized

genitalia erupting to seraphic red
skulls which disembodied hands
wrenched wailing into glare.
So it is, on nights when my tongue

laves the bud, my broaching prayer
at a salvatory gate, I reel
again through shuttered puberty
to face those scalpels wielded at the groin.

❦

THE BURNING OF TROY

The opals the shopclerk tweezed
between her lacquered nails
flashed with such agitation
I knew the young fiancés
could never afford any stone
she floated before their eyes.
Even her jeweler's terms
to describe shifting auroral
patterns seemed neon buzz
meant more to dazzle unlikely
prospects than define
infinite illusory depths:
fan harlequins, peacock
tails, chaff and straw,
a mackerel sky roiling
with rarest sunset reds—
"much like Napoleon's gift
to Josephine, *The Burning
of Troy*." Then sizing them up,
she let the boy hold
a boulder opal from a Queensland
field (even the name,
Jundah, jumped with fire
from her tongue): She explained
the hidden veins beneath
the outback scrub the dozers
had to peel away like skin,
the mullock heaps, the pickaxed
scars, the faint hopes
sparking with each chisel
blow, till that shard chanced
to split, and the dust-light
shuddered into fire: two carats
cut to the rough contours
of the underlying iron-

stone which cupped the glaze,
so thin the brown rock
bled through in part like a bruise.
Still, from where I stood
nearby, I glimpsed a myriad
of splintered lights charging
that tiny dollop in his
callused palm. How useless,
I thought, my staring into
its frozen turbulence.
What smoldering conquests of mine
could match what he was now
imagining captured in that blaze?
For burning such as his,
I once laid waste
a citadel, spent all I had.

PASSOVER

Today a northering flock of waxwings squalled
through the privet, tore the last black beads of winter-
shriveled fruit from its tattered brocade, then splintered
off through still-bare oaks.

                    Their high, thin calls
trickled down the frozen hollow of my being,
the soul-haunt where the broad conflicted world's
writ small. I stood at my window, facing those pearled
lights of evening, for comfort, yes,

                        but seeing
their flux in the hedgerow, then sudden absence there
widening like a bruise, I hunkered back inside
my narrow grief, though many this day, I know, have died
of terror, tankfire, cancer, long despair,
the bitter pity of the self-content,
in want of even that small sacrament.

THE CONVERGENCE

How to live with disaster's after-
image, the brain blazed with it
but nevertheless unbruising,

the body of it, going
cold?—as if at first, clouds,
then the cast lid

of them, raindrops
into rivulets, and then—
how long after?—

the slow or long
drainage into dry
forgottenness:

to be able to say,
it rained, but not
precisely recalling

when, now the sky
sheens with soulless
indifference. Are we not each

alone in our common grief
though we'd have it verge,
lest it stay disaster, a life deluged—

but look, that shoal of menhaden
the striped bass slices through:
their unschooled flight that so

stips the cove *is* the condition
toward which any vital fear
instinctively educates

—and here, the ant nest
the spade ravages,
and the one writhing

at a distance, underfoot:
in equal, if unproportionable,
pain.

RESOLVE

I'll put aside those images, the camcorded
streaks, for already I bear the raised, raw
welt, the thrust fiery brand of grief hard
upon the brain. I'll listen past the thunder
of gray blossoms bursting from the ground,
the snuffed cries deep within each petal's
heavy folds, for souls too fast are silent,
light as pollen in the air, and I
would hear them again, breathe them in again
though my lungs are full to aching. But how ignore
the Babel of opinion mounted stone by stone
that forever comes crashing into our lives
like vengeance? Better, I'll say, to think on where
that travel-weary Samaritan crouches
now, amid what rubble of the world,
faintly calling through the terror. The words
lodge like barbs on my tongue: *And who is my neighbor?*

A man who's memorized π
out to the 2600th decimal place
is joking with the radio announcer
about the uncanny stretch
of his mind, while I, bathed
in the dashboard's radium glow,
feel myself begin to hurtle faster
as the thought of π hits me like a wind-
driven mote of dust about to lodge
against the eye—an unproportionate
irritant, like an idea of God—
and I become that thought
and plummet deep inside a pitch-
black gaze, an unblinking logic
beyond reason.
           It's how I imagine
that overwintering flock of monarchs,
storm-caught in remote Mexican highlands:
the whole orange-black amalgam
plucked one by one from trees,
the slo-mo flutter as they fall stunned
through freezing air, the insistent
replication till hundreds of millions
drift in foot-deep piles across
the forest floor.
           It's how on nights
when I try to count my way
toward some solace in the world
and spin out my scant powers to the limit,
I always fall short somewhere this side
of sleep, feeling the chill that resides
even within such paltry finitude.
           It's how

the settled blanket of those wings,
its radiant and measurable acreage,
is enough to suffocate under.

❧

CHAPELLE DU ROSAIRE, VENCE

> *. . . il apportera la guérison dans son rayonnement.*
> —Malachi 3:20

Even though to bask in the elemental
winter light of Matisse's chapel
I had to grope for sense as I stumbled
through the Dominicans' Mass in French—
as if it were a transmission beamed
through solar storm, with so much lost
in synaptic static—still I could give thanks
for that cloudless day, the broad stain

of the glass eddying forth earthly yellows,
blues, and greens over the congregants
and floor, the colors' rising to affront
the opposite austere and white-
tiled walls, where the artist had swabbed
the outlines of the patron saint in his robes,
the Virgin and Child in a clouded sky—
all faceless, in pure black strokes.

Was it balance he sought, or battle,
some final gloss on art's ascendancy—
to say, perhaps, those glyphs of distant divinity
must be imbued with fickle play,
the splatter of the world's indifference, to seem
even remotely worthy of our attention?
I tried to understand, but the priest's words
droned like gnats at my ears, and I mumbled

prayers, now forgotten, while there, beyond
the altar, Matisse's Tree of Life, a blue-
stemmed cactus like the "vigorous stroke
of a gong," ablaze with skygold blooms

on a green field, eclipsed the ritual passing
before it: all the dogma of drought and thorns
and the radiant shroud seemed filtered through
his trinity of colored panes in channeled lead.

Mass done, I lingered, while the faithful
drained from the nave. The midday light,
now grown intense, suffused the narrow space.
An aged nun, who seemed to have stepped out
of the facing wall, hovered near, her habit
fully submerged and at home within
that reef of shifting lights, which instead
had made my skin appear bruised,

flush with the random wash of a student's
aquarelle. And I realized it wasn't balance
I'd sought, nor comfort nor any semblance
of sacrament or grace, but the stagecraft
of a director, hidden in the wings,
the sun itself a prop, the earth a flywheel
for the rising curtain, and Matisse himself
crouched at the floods, slipping in

the cellophane gels. With waning patience
the nun, who'd endured five decades
of my kind, gently began to usher me out.
As I glanced a last time at those windows,
a blinding blue shaft hooked me in the eye,
but I forced myself, though I'd turned away
in pain, to look back, now through tears,
into what I felt was a knowing stare.

❦

BEHIND THE COLOR OF THINGS

Čimelice Castle

This morning I found five fledgling swallows
from the night before, frantic, unwearying
for open dawn. The high-ceilinged room
where they'd perched on a cornice ledge

combusted with trapped energy, the pitched
Morse of their calls, till I flung the casements wide,
and with one last centrifugal loop, they rocketed
toward insect-studded light: "living fireworks,"

that's what I read just minutes later, sitting
over coffee, right where I'd left off with Proust
—Vol. II, p. 444—at Balbec, his swallows there
above the sea's "long horizontal wakes,"

the "charming miracle" of those birds charming me
with coincidence till I felt swept along the blurred
trail of what so recently was, among turns
and sallies of an inexhaustible prose, time's ocean

spread beyond a window, into which everything
sinks: Sunday morning cyclers, the distant
engine-whine of transport, even the hawthorns applauding
the momentary wind. "My mind . . . ," he wrote,

"was incapable of putting any depth behind
the color of things"—as here—except for those flecks
and daubs on the canvas of being, their scissoring
wings, tails forked then flared, each swerve and weave

a "necessary connection" to define a space worthy
of our small lives, as if it were a work
under continuous revision, a syntax
always in search of that final ellipsis.

❧

A FIELD IN BOHEMIA

A marker plots the old geometry,
redrawn atop the latest property lines:

a square jackknifing to a right triangle,
the ragtag buildings sketched-in, numbered,

and keyed to the necessary legend: Isolation,
Disinfection, Delousing, Deratization.

And so in steps, three hundred twenty-seven
Gypsies died, another five eleven crated off

to Auschwitz—such precision in those numbers,
abstractions that almost obliterate what we can't

see and yet survey to pin it down as history. Here
the State demarcates the garden of its mean regret:

a tract of waste between a barley field
and a row of barns that slurry the sun-washed

Bohemian air with the pungent slop of pigs—
all left unchecked, where weeds now outnumber

any counting, their flowerings useless as lost souls,
till in the not-forgetting we might recall their curative

lore: that yellow mulleins' woolly leaves, dipped
in rationed drops of fat, once served as lampwicks,

that nettles' prickly stems can be boiled for soup
and yarrows brewed to ease the ache of unrelenting

sorrow. To tread among the camomiles,
toadflax, and thistles, the lupines' patches

of blued earth, the wild carrots' fragile lace,
is to know at last that we, too, trample

the unruly litany of outcast names.
Their profusions cluster like gaudy caravans

for the dead. So let the scattering seed-winds
tend what we must neglect.

A YOUNG HORSEMAN IN THE CAMARGUE

He rode into view, all rumbling thunder,
bare-chested, bronzed, yet little more
than a boy atop the gelding's bellows-flare.

Like combers rolling in from the sea, the sheer
dare and thrill of him carried me in their sweep
as he hunkered to the animal's heaving

crest, the thin arms stretched to their limit
around the brindled neck, and I knew
that gallop would soon outpace his prowess,

that slick flanks must sap a boy's
clamped thighs, and the two-as-one
fall out of sync. And yes, he was spun

to the sand, lay there dazed while his mount,
no longer compelled by heel and crop, grazed
on dune grass, mighty in its indifference.

How does one plummet with purpose,
approach again an overshadowing,
unbridled force? Before I could reach him,

the boy had stood, unbroken, and I thought
I glimpsed the youth that I had been,
or wanted to be, gripping a frenzied mane

that seemed at once blast-furnace white
and glacial as a page, and I remembered
that broodmare twitched with attention

when I first whispered in its ear—as if
into the din of chaos, beyond all fear or falling—
how I wanted to haul our weight into air.

ONE YEAR AFTER

Vauvenargues

Hang gliders soar on radiant thermals
in the easing August light of Mont Ste-Victoire.

For all the apparent daintiness, a switchback
logic underpins their lustrous flight and risk.

Any moment they may cascade down the saint's
scarped and skull-white face. I prefer to think

of Calders than the colder, more highly wrought
steel of courage such enthusiasts embody.

Soon they'll sink to safety with the cooling sun
as it casts its dark net across the valley

till up and up it grips the terrace where I'll sit
as it trawls the sky of lingering blue and the faint

chirps and squeaks begin within the overlapping
barrel-vaulted tiles: a reveille of bats above my head.

One by one they'll dollop down and arc off in erratic
quests. Their crescent wings will sound like

silks dredged gently over startled skin. And suddenly
it will be as if he's here, my love, like a static charge

in the frisson of a thought—this thought
that I am writing here, between these counterweights

of dusk: a fulcrum between warring forces that yet
might sprout wings and loft beyond this twilit page.

CANTICLE FOR A.

For hours now I've tried to imagine
that final sinking, drunk into the mattress,
a cigarette's sloughed skin, its red bead

slinking through floral bedding, the slow
smolder like venom, the years
we didn't speak, and tonight this searing

news. And tonight, as on another, I'd bend
to the body's worship, penitent, lacking
in grace, and devoutly count the Aves

of a spine, then kneel in the aching
flesh that never can transcend
such frailties, this pilgrim's mortified path

toward no absolving state, unless it's
here, in a single sainted choir,
all past love still burns.

III

—Earth! invisible!
What, if not transformation, is your urgent command?
—Rilke

. . . I have become rich
with disappearance. I have become this light . . .
—Betty Adcock

FOSSIL STONE FROM
GREEN RIVER SHALES, WYOMING

Knightia eocenica

This slab's an inland sea
for twenty-one ray-finned
fish, their skeletons

incused, a spawning shoal
caught in as much of forever
as this world affords. Delicate

ghostings of the Eocene,
mounted and lit on a facing
wall, they bear the finish

of art, iconic against
the sand-colored stone,
streaked with yellow ochre,

suggesting depths and not
the quiet catastrophic
bloom that sluiced the oxygen

from their gills, left them to rot,
flat in the shallows till the press
of time released them swimming

here, compassed in all directions—
a trick on the willing eye
as if the mouths still gape for air.

❧

TREE KANGAROO

Dendrolagus goodfellowi

Within the cramped enclosure, its clutch
of low plantings meant to hint
at native Papuan range—some upland
density—she hunkers, nose
to paws, on a bare wood plank mounted
above the humble canopy,

                      like an anchorite
bent to the ceaseless curve of meditation,
as if she could see in looking down
at her forelegs' pink-clawed stars
the limbs of that ancestral other
who scruffed the earth a million years
ago and willed herself unbound,

                      and bounded
skyward, the hindtoes hooking there
to complications she'd not foreseen
amid the totter of trees: an uncadenced life,
ever verging on collapse back
to what was left behind: the desire
or deformity that sparked the leap.

❧

IN THE STYX RIVER VALLEY

Maydena Range, Tasmania

The guide claimed the water safe
though stained with the brew of fallen
old-growth eucalypts and ferns.
On the shaded bank, we shed
our clothes and stepped across
the riverstones, inching our bodies
deep in the chilling flow. *Hades,*

Dis—the names sprang from the eroded
bedrock of our high-school Greek,
steeped as we were in the Dead's
constant girding. After, we climbed
the valley, up toward blackened acres
where we'd heard an ancient stand had been
clear-felled, and stood at the edge

of that sun-struck overworld,
amazed at the massive stumps
and mangled waste—napalmed,
bulldozed flat, then laced with poison
carrots to cull any possum or potoroo
that might forage among the new-sown
sapling rows. Before we could turn away,

a pair of wedge-tailed eagles dived
into that mauled and nurtured square.
Like salvagers on a beached wreck,
they hauled out stowed rigging: slick,
orange-pocked, marsupial innards.
When the birds soared to their nest of sticks,
the coils glinted in their beaks like gold.

MOURNING CUTTLEFISH

Sepia plangon

The eyes looked human, irises blue
(like mine), the pupils deep as wells,

but registered a doleful awareness:
that they'd seen thousands such as me

schooling past. —He wavered
amid the endless peristalsis

of his fins, blimpish and benign,
like one sent up for life who's learned

to wear confinement as the skin
he can no longer shed. My face,

I thought, must seem just any other
image drifting beyond his grasp

of need or bodily hunger. He stared
and pursed his tentacles a moment

against the glass, the tips tickling
at some combination, then let them flare.

In one chromatic blink, all
but his eyes became familiar pattern—

the repetitive, florid, sun-faded tropic
of the shirt I wore. It withered as quick

as he into doubt. Then rigid with fear,
he fled in a squirt of ink and turned

a gash of russet gold to hide
within a tangled strop of kelp.

I peered across that near divide
as if the eons had collapsed

to form a brief transparency,
till foolish for some small reprieve

my fingers rose, less tender
than tentative, to touch the glass.

LORETTA'S PEACOCKS

"As bad as those immigrants," Gabe, my sister's neighbor spouts,
"or worse," pointing to the dozen squiggly slugs of peafowl
excrement that slick the entry walk. "Where'd they all
come from anyway?" Imperious, in the full pride
of breeding plumage, the specimen under discussion
gazes down from a pine bough ten feet overhead.
His furled tail's blank and blazing eyes, inscrutably at ease,
seem instead to scrutinize us, eye to eye. The real cause
of crisis: his prim-crested peahen who's nestled drably
again at the front door, among the brighter birds
of paradise in the foundation planter. "They've eaten all
the impatiens," Loretta complains. "There's not a lobelia left,
and look—the ground's all scratched up in their search for grubs."
"At least there are no grubs," I quip and can't help imagining
those stolen petals mashed in the birds' gizzards
till each pigment's distilled and somehow transubstantiated
into a sanctity of colored feathers. "When she's off the nest,"
Gabe points, "take the eggs. She'll then move on."

That night we awake to the peacocks' chilling clarions
and lie frozen under siege as . . . what?—coyote pack?
a wildcat from the hills?—stalks the neighborhood.
Come morning, my sister's had enough of ruckus.
Her house cat coils and nuzzles at her legs as she talks.
"I'll do what Gabe suggests." On the pavement we find
one egg, cracked, a casualty of skirmish, its morsel gone.
Nearby, paying no mind, the jug-round peahen lumbers,
probes the dichondra lawn. In her nest, we find four remaining
powdery pale, warm eggs, one for each of our palms, and bear
those suspended lives back into the kitchen, where Loretta places
each handful on a separate freezer shelf. At the dull kiss
of the door's rubber gasket against the metal, I sense
neither right nor wrong, but a simple stewardship,
a necessity to survive in a land forever alien, that we'd have

for home. But, dear sister, now that we surviving
children of immigrants are ourselves generationless, what
unpredicted wildness can we hope will fan out in our wakes?

❧

ANTARCTIC PRION

Pachyptila desolata

The way its neck lolled in the water's shallow give
and take, I'd presumed it dead, a derelict nestling,

or beachdrift washed up after storm,
but then an eye twitched skyward,

angling toward what gaped there, a shadow
stooping like a child above a kite, afraid to touch

lest touching damage more a shattered thing.
Still I scooped it up, a palmful of dust-

blue feathers at the surge-end of the tide,
and held it into the squalled light,

passive to the wind, and watched
the fine-edged, perfect blades snap wide,

desolation's last few unspent ounces
again magisterial, nearing that ideal of air-

y nothing, till the exquisite frame lofted
almost from my hand, as if intent

alone could fuel a life of yet more
wandering. What didn't I already know

of teeming vacancy, the uncountable
miles already flown—necessary, uncaring

space far beyond that exposed stretch
on the Tasman Sea—where I left that bird on the sand?

LOBSTER-CLAWS

Heliconia bihai

The gift at my door held me a moment in windless
heat, as if the tropics had honed those red
pendant-stemmed bracts into claws,

but when I slid the card from its sheath, I felt
the cold advance and sudden rush
of what they signified: a cut

bouquet of condolences, long after the fact,
and with them came the underscuttle,
clamp and inescapable crush

of remembrance. Centered on the bare
dining-room table, they seemed
imperious as staves of state,

primitive, battle-smeared blades
meant to humble any gaze,
so I sat bowed in tearful

anger till I began to see, looking
up at the cleft tip of each,
minuscule yellow-

lipped petals cradling beads
of intensest blue—all
the hard armature

of those exotic growths
devolved, seeded
there, in flame.

NOCTILUCA

Port Douglas, Queensland

I'd not forgiven the loss, the rasp
of dream, a throat raw in the repeated
waking to tears like iron filings,
my body awash in a half-life

of grievance. If chaos is the pattern
too vast to comprehend, except to sense
in it a sneer, the ocean that night,
its near liquescence, the breakers' far

rumbles across the reef seemed syllables
shaping an utterance that receded
to dark just at the verge of grasping.
Isn't this what I wanted, the world

to gather that discordance toward
a steady pulse, the tide, oncoming,
to rise toward some resonant *Amen*,
to say, *Enough of this?* The sky

was moonless when I walked calf-deep
in the dissolving surf, its sound
my footsteps' only guide till that wavering
path began to gleam from within,

a snaking into light, and I could see
my ankles sparking like struck flint,
and I sank, as if abrading away,
into the to-and-fro of wonder:

An invisible surround of life speckled
my chest and thighs with Kirlian aura,
my trawling hands trailed comet tails,
pale turbulences in the blood-

warm sea, which as quick ebbed off,
and all about again went dark.
—"Quite common," the hotel staff
explained next morning, "luminescent

plankton feeding among the shallows"—
which left, I suppose, room enough
for further miracle and tears,
till the Aborigine I questioned

said I'd bathed in the spent excess
of the Rainbow Serpent's sperm,
so that when the glow of his so distant
Dreaming left me to stub my way

back to the waiting bed, I could know
finally through those tears that this
is how the spirit shines, if it must shine
at all, at the body's awful going.

KATA TJUTA

Amadeus Basin, Northern Territory

The blood-light of recent rain
had stippled the path, obliterating
any human trace through the gorge.
Where I snaked along the base
into the center of those clustered domes,

flowers pulsed against the blush
and burn of the rockface. The dry earth
was hastily alive again with silver-tails,
shrubby mulgas, bristling hummocks
of spinifex, the unbrittled froth

of gnarled acacias. It seemed a stringent
landscape's whittled perfection, not
a "ghastly blank" (as Europeans dubbed
that desert), but a deathless space
of uncompromising magnanimity.

Still it's impossible to trek there now
and not think of civilization's overtowering
extremes—a city's massive windowed heights—
or to step even briefly out of geologic
time, knowing a quarter mile skyward

the world eroded and left those "many heads"
hobnobbing above the ferrous plain.
The first Aborigines to pass among them
possessed no notion or need of mortared polity;
the rocks spoke through embering dusks

in languages preutterant as wind
till stories spilled like runnels from the summits
down to lustering pools and told

how here creation dreamt itself into being.
Who wouldn't want to see the gods in everything,

to stammer through that visual syntax
time and again like a liturgy for the living
and the dead, and read in the soil's tiniest
quickenings, in the slow accretion or seismic
upheaval of our days a cartography of the soul—

and so hold onto every swift-perishing
grace? —That day I glimpsed a peregrine
as it tore through the gorge. That fast,
then gone. In the wake of its scree,
I craned toward emptiness, into savaged blue,

waiting, while all around me the furrowed slopes
slid gently into flame. Minutes, more, I stood
as if eye to eye, consumed—so dazzling
was the world's annihilating glance—till finally
I doubled back along the ruined trail,

where my earlier boot-prints now brimmed
with shadows. And so we shoulder what little
history we have, like an aged parent
through burning streets, with love's small store
packed in a rucksack alongside our bearable

load of sorrows. Isn't this all the myth we need
for the journey out into the inevitable,
unsheltering dark? —not so much to relive
the momentary arc above the heart's red center,
the wounding absence of that raptor-split sky,

but to bless somehow the plod through
each day's exile and return, the meandering
path, the thin scar we blindly finger
through the night, whereby we trace
at last our only healing.

TIGER SNAKE

Notechis scutatus

The cloacal slit was ruptured tire-wide,
and in the chancel of that wound blowflies
thrummed. But even curled at the curb, with the slick
trail so evident across the road—
a sign of the lash and lunge for distant cover—
that limp rope kept its meter's worth
of venom, enough to cause a recoil from
its dead-on stare.

        Other dusks, I'd seen them
—solitary, molten streams in the sure
swerve of indirection—staggered at their crossings,
caught beneath my headlight's blaze and the hit-
or-miss of a moment's hesitancy to brake
or push the pedal down. The rearview
would show a fleeting snap of what: mere fright
or fatal agony? I never knew.

        And there,
as I stooped, adrenaline-charged, half-guarded
by fear, above that bluntly resolute head,
its vacant gaze snaked like fire through my veins.
Long into the night I saw how to make a way.

CAIRNS BIRDWING

Ornithoptera priamus euphorion

Thirty miles out, east of Opal Reef,
where we'd spent the day snorkeling,
a cloudbank suddenly flared above
the patinating sea. And idly, I imagined
a city's towers massed against the sky
and felt a heart-rush like splendor
before that image of consuming flame,

then came the pin-prick of a thought:
Was it beauty I'd kindled with that spark?
So when a handspan of black, green and golden
iridescence fluttered across the deck—
alighting nowhere, vigorous in its fragility
far from forest shelter—and winged off
out into the open Pacific toward that dying

brilliance, I shuddered for what I knew
was lost: Priam again "with Troy in flames
before his eyes, his towers headlong fallen."
Yet as we churned back to port in the ash
of evening and the image of that insect dwindled
to a mirage and a name, from within the taxa
of its being a euphoric wisdom began to burn.

ꔵ

THE THEFT

When I looked back on those lost
cities, their architecture at last
grim-ghosted, I imagined me
there, still, in a semblance of
an ideal, not in some future
present, the unbowered barrow
our flesh had been trudging toward,

but timeless, perfect, always
amid shifting angularities
of light, a demarcated dark,
the edge between, half-veiling
my face as once before when I turned
—if now only in the thought of it—
toward his to thieve a kiss.

❧

SMOKE TREE

Cotinus coggygria

I was hiking half a world from home
when I saw a smoke tree on the trail ahead
smolder into a lather of light, plush
as powder in the heat-choked air—

and clustered along spinules, thin
as capillaries, a tiny arson flared,
then rose into a stratosphere
where the ash of all I was and had

was rushing toward some distant ground
I'd planted once with such as this
in memory of someone dead, and from
that half a world away, a cloud returned

faltering with rain: I was no longer sad.

SATIN BOWERBIRD BLUES

Ptilinorhynchus violaceus

When whatever tripwire
triggers his compulsion,
he constructs a U from twigs

and hoop-pine needles tapered
foot-high at the tips
like horns. To this courtyard

of bliss he brings the bluest
trophies he can find
to entice the demurely dull-

green bowerhens
to his violaceous eyes—
blues electric and ultra-

marine: swap-shop gems,
wrapper scraps and straws,
a plastic bottlecap. His is craft

cerulean, lapis, indican
to swell a heart like a sapphire
star till he bursts into a fluff-

'n-ruffle jig with a navy
clothespeg, perhaps, in his bill.
Whether an audience will come

and stay, enthralled, he breaks
—guttural, glissando—
into pure cyanic song.

STEPPING OUTSIDE, WE LOOK AT MARS

August 27, 2003

Not red, certainly, more the startle of
terra cotta bled through an heirloom's black
glaze. Or the spent, sweet stains of this
evening's port in our glasses, left there inside
amid the rubble of the dinner table.
Or the spark that once studded another's ear,
now far, yet seeming proximate. Alone,
I'd whisper some words up from this ravaged planet
—so luminous and doomed—some emberings
born of wonder—and consign them to the hiss
of space, toward that calculable spin, that other
atmosphere I'd never expect or want
to wake in. They'd hold a moment's significance
perhaps, become themselves sublime specks.
How fast that world recedes. Arm in arm
we turn to see our candles guttered, the room
grown dark, then, more fiercely, bright again.

BATS ROOSTING AT SYDNEY BOTANIC GARDENS

Pteropus poliocephalus

If I could resist surmise,
I'd read nothing in the heart
of things, those dark sacks
that have stripped the upmost
branches and splotched the path
with musky excrement.
Instead I stare into black
chrysalides of noon, hanging
like tarot's condemned, feet
noosed heavenward, heads
plumbed and draped not, I know,
in shame, but with forbearance,
weary as any beneath this sun.
A few, like Lenten congregants
thrumming mea culpas, quaver
an outer wing, restless for relief.
Others stoke the air with sheening
lateen sails rigged on thinnest
finger-spars, the muscle-stumps
for arms clear against the light.
It is what lies within, shrouded now,
the alienate core, that frightens,
dormant, indifferent, how at dusk,
with the city's shimmer quickening,
they'll drop on cue and soar
up from the coward bottom
of the human brain—*sursum
corda*—and embrace so easefully
what they've always known
as theirs, the immense negative
that somehow holds the stars in place.

FLAME

I don't want to think about anything,
except to become language.
                              —Stanley Kunitz

Once again the poppies:
I'd stay the wind to keep
their pure scorch, this
conflagration thrusting
up from mulish roots
despite years of my spade's
accidental loppings.

This morning it seemed a hundred
crimson Hydra heads
rose through the seadrift fog,
the kind of monstrous beauty
we demand of myth in the aftermath
of winter. That's the problem,
isn't it: the splendid seduction

of these Salomes, what they unveil
in stages, the black intent
they keep hidden till the end
within scrolled parchments,
the taunting logic we can't help
thoughtlessly lusting after,
and would, at a stroke, become,

even as the leaves drift
toward jaundice beneath
brittle, rattling pods.

MOON JELLYFISH

Aurelia aurita

No planet could keep so many moons in tow.
They drift, constantly unconstellating
around you in their milky way. Even to want

to cradle one in your palm would compromise
their elegance: the opaque domes
are stippled with a compass rose and trail,

like auroras, fine voluted veils. Gravity
would spell their deaths. Voiceless, blind,
they seem oracular—mouths and eyes

fixed since the first pulse of the world's womb
on a source beyond orbits of perception. To swim
among them is to float as if in the pure *We are*

that scorched the oceans into life. Watch
how your mere expended breath, on its own
celestial path, must break into their midst.

NOTES

"Aubade": In Apuleius' famous tale, Psyche is unaware her lover is the god Cupid, who visits her only in absolute darkness and forbids her ever to gaze upon him. Each dawn she finds herself alone. Eventually fearing he may be a monstrous serpent, she resolves to kill him in his sleep, but Cupid awakes when burning oil from her lamp drips onto his skin. The wounded god then deserts Psyche, precipitating her long despair and quest for reconciliation. Beneath all the frivolity and burlesque that colors Apuleius' "fairy bridegroom" tale lies an allegory of the soul's stumbling persistence to achieve union with divine beauty: that perfect, unseen other.

"A Pot of Crocuses": The women of ancient Athens celebrated the death and resurrection of Adonis in an annual springtime festival, during which they set out on their rooftops small pots of forced flowers. Because these "Adonis gardens" would soon wither under the heat of the April sun, the expression eventually was used to refer to any transitory pleasure.

"Samsara": "That wheel, / that gap" literally refers to a dark nebula near the Southern Cross known as the Coal Sack, which appears as a blank space within the surrounding brilliance of the Milky Way, giving the illusion of a round window opened onto nothingness.

"Cowrie": The "life-sized sculpture" is a reference to the famous Borghese *Sleeping Hermaphrodite* in the Louvre and similar works that appear entirely male only when viewed from a precise angle.

"Among the Daughters of Lycomedes": Thetis, knowing that her son Achilles would die at Troy, dressed him as a girl and took him to Scyros to be raised among King Lycomedes' daughters, but Odysseus discovered the hidingplace and tricked Achilles into revealing his disguise. In Ovid's *Metamorphoses*, Odysseus recalls the incident:

> "I said, 'Son of a goddess, Troy is damned;
> She waits for you to rape her, tear her down.

What are you waiting for? That great doomed city trembles
For you to enter her and take her falling ruins.'
With this, I put my hand upon his arm,
And sent the hero to heroic duties."   (tr. Horace Gregory)

The irony of Odysseus' boasting is that Achilles is already dead and fell before the city did.

"Poolside in Provincetown": "Gomorrah" alludes to Operation Gomorrah, the Allies' code name for the firebombing of Hamburg on July 28, 1943.

"The Burning of Troy": In giving the splendid opal to Josephine, Napoleon was symbolically declaring her his Helen of Troy. Legend has it she promptly lost the gem.

"A Field in Bohemia": The lack of a formal memorial at Lety is as much the result of local controversy over whether Czechs rather than Nazis manned the concentration camp as it is of on-going, institutionalized discrimination against Gypsies.

"In the Styx River Valley": According to Forestry Tasmania, "Although secondary poisoning may occur when a carnivorous animal ingests the carcass of an animal previously killed by 1080 poison baits, current research reveals that native carnivores such as . . . wedge-tailed eagles are not killed by eating the carcasses of animals killed by 1080" (*The Sunday Tasmanian*, Feb. 11, 2001). Owing to such logic, fewer than two hundred nesting pairs of wedge-tailed eagles remain on the island.

"Noctiluca": literally, "night-shining," an epithet of the Roman moon goddess. Dinoflagellates, which share the traits of both plants and animals, are responsible for most of the bioluminescence found in the seas. Among Australian Aborigines, the Creator or Rainbow Serpent—at times male, at times female—is "the most potent expression of Deity . . . throughout the continent" (James Cowan, *Mysteries of the Dreaming*, Brandl & Schlesinger, 2001). A universal chthonic presence, the snake, in Aboriginal tradition, is the Truth-revealer, associated with lightning and spiritual illumination.

"Kata Tjuta": literally, "Many Heads," until recently more commonly known as the Olgas. This massive outcropping in the central Australian desert, like its more famous neighbor Uluru (Ayers Rock) is sacred to the region's Aborigines, who believe the Rainbow Serpent resides in a pool atop the tallest dome. According to Cowan, the Aborigines in their seasonal treks over the course of the millennia created "a metaphysical edifice" of the land, "a visual language . . . out of rocks, contours, flora, fauna" that enabled them to "re-create the eternal moment of the Dreaming," so that by journeying through their environment they were able to encounter "their entire past existing integrally in their present."

It was Thales who said "the gods are in everything."

The "aged parent" is a reference to Anchises, who was carried from Troy on Aeneas' shoulders.

"Cairns Birdwing": The quotation from Book II of *The Aeneid* is Robert Fitzgerald's translation.

ACKNOWLEDGMENTS

My thanks to the editors of the following publications in which these poems previously appeared:

Alabama Literary Review: "Aix en Provence," "A Field in Bohemia," "Flame," and "A Young Horseman in the Camargue";

Arts & Letters: "Smoke" and "Smoke Tree";

Barrow Street: "Yorke Woods";

Boulevard: "Bats Roosting at Sydney Botanic Gardens," "Behind the Color of Things," "Fossil Stone from Green River Shales, Wyoming," and "Tiger Snake";

The Café Review: "Among the Daughters of Lycomedes";

Connecticut Review: "Cairns Birdwing";

Inkwell: "Octet";

Iron Horse Literary Review: "Aubade," "Chapelle du Rosaire, Vence," "In Dream," "Loretta's Peacocks," "Marionette," and "A Pot of Crocuses";

Island (Australia): "Antarctic Prion," "Noctiluca," and "Satin Bowerbird Blues";

Kestrel: "In the Styx River Valley," "Mourning Cuttlefish," and "Training Film, 1967";

Lake Effect: "Artichoke";

Maine in Print: "An Abiding" and "π";

MARGIE: "Canticle for A.";

Mid-American Review: "Cowrie";

The National Poetry Review: "Stone";

New England Review: "The Burning of Troy";

Pen World International: "Early and Late";

Pleiades: "Poolside in Provincetown";

Poems & Plays: "One Year After";

Prairie Schooner: "Minotaur," "Setting Out," and "Spoons";

Rattapallax: "Drum";

Shenandoah: "Vigil";

The Southern Review: "Lobster-Claws," "Moon Jellyfish," and "Tree Kangaroo";

Southwest Review: "The Theft";

Tar River Poetry: "Stepping Outside, We Look at Mars";

The Texas Review: "Passover";

TriQuarterly: "Kata Tjuta," "Samsara," and "Winter Solstice: Newgrange, Ireland";

Verse: "Tithonus";

The York Independent: "Resolve."

"An Abiding" is reprinted, with one small change, from my earlier collection *Double Going* (BOA Editions, 2002).

"Resolve" was reprinted in the anthology *September 11, 2001: American Writers Respond*, edited by William Heyen (Etruscan Press, 2002).

Many of the poems in this book were written during a period spent abroad as the Amy Lowell Poetry Travelling Scholar for 2000/2001. My deepest gratitude to the judges and administrators of this award.

I am also grateful for a 2004 Good Idea Grant from the Maine Arts Commission, which allowed me to travel.

My thanks to Eamon Grennan for selecting "Octet" as the winner of the 2004 *Inkwell* Poetry Competition and to Betty Adcock for permission to use an excerpt from her poem "Clearing Out, 1974."

Special thanks to the many artist retreats and people who nurtured me in body and spirit during the writing of this book, especially Varuna: The Writers' House in Katoomba, New South Wales; the Tasmanian Writers' Centre and the Hobart City Council for the grant of a 2002 Residency for an International Writer; the Tyrone Guthrie Centre at Annaghmakerrig, Ireland; Čimelice Castle and the Foundation and Center for Contemporary Arts—Prague; Laure-Anne Bosselaar and Kurt Brown for "Carpe Diem"; the La Napoule Arts Foundation, Mandelieu-La Napoule, France; and DRC.

ABOUT THE AUTHOR

Richard Foerster was born in the Bronx, New York, and has worked as a lexicographer, educational writer, typesetter, teacher and as the editor of the literary magazine *Chelsea*. He is the author of four previous collections: *Sudden Harbor* and *Patterns of Descent* (both published by Orchises Press); *Trillium* (BOA Editions, 1998), which received Honorable Mention for the 2000 Poets' Prize; and *Double Going* (BOA, 2002). Other honors include the "Discovery"/*The Nation* Award, *Poetry* magazine's Bess Hokin Prize, fellowships from the National Endowment for the Arts and the Maine Arts Commission, the 2000/2001 Amy Lowell Poetry Travelling Scholarship, and the 2002 Hobart City Council Residency for an International Writer. He currently lives in York Beach, Maine, and edits *Chautauqua Literary Journal*.

❧

BOA EDITIONS, LTD.
AMERICAN POETS CONTINUUM SERIES

COLOPHON

The Burning of Troy, poems by Richard Foerster, is set in Goudy, a digital variation of the font originally developed in 1916 by Frederic W. Goudy (1865–1947) for American Type Founders. Considered an American master of type design, Goudy created more than one hundred typefaces during his career. The cover art, "The Burning of Troy," by Jan Brueghel the Elder (1568–1625), is from the Alte Pinakothek in Munich, courtesy of ARTOTHEK. The cover design is by Geri McCormick. Manufacturing is by BookMobile, Minneapolis, Minnesota.

❦

The publication of this book is made possible, in part, by the special support of the following individuals:

E. Thomas Babineau, Jr.
Alan & Nancy Cameros
Loretta H. Casey
Gwen & Gary Conners
Dennis Czajkowski
Peter & Suzanne Durant
Bev & Pete French
Dane & Judy Gordon
Kip & Deb Hale
Peter & Robin Hursh
Robert & Willy Hursh
X. J. Kennedy
Archie & Pat Kutz
Rosemary & Lew Lloyd
Jimmy & Wendy Mnookin
Alan & Sylvia Newman
Boo Poulin
Mary J. Simpson
Michael Waters
Pat & Michael Wilder